First published by Walker Books Ltd in
Bear's Birthday (1985), *Help!* (1985),
Jumping (1985), *Make a Face* (1985),
Shirley's Shops (1986) and *So Can I* (1985)

This edition published 1997

Text © 1985, 1986 Allan Ahlberg
Illustrations © 1985, 1986 Colin McNaughton

This book has been typeset in ITC Garamond Light.

Printed in Hong Kong

British Library Cataloguing in Publication Data
A catalogue record for this book is available
from the British Library.

ISBN 0-7445-4980-9

A RED NOSE COLLECTION

WHAT'S IN THE SHOP?

Allan Ahlberg + Colin McNaughton

WALKER BOOKS
AND SUBSIDIARIES
LONDON • BOSTON • SYDNEY

PUSH AND PULL

pull and push

push

and pull

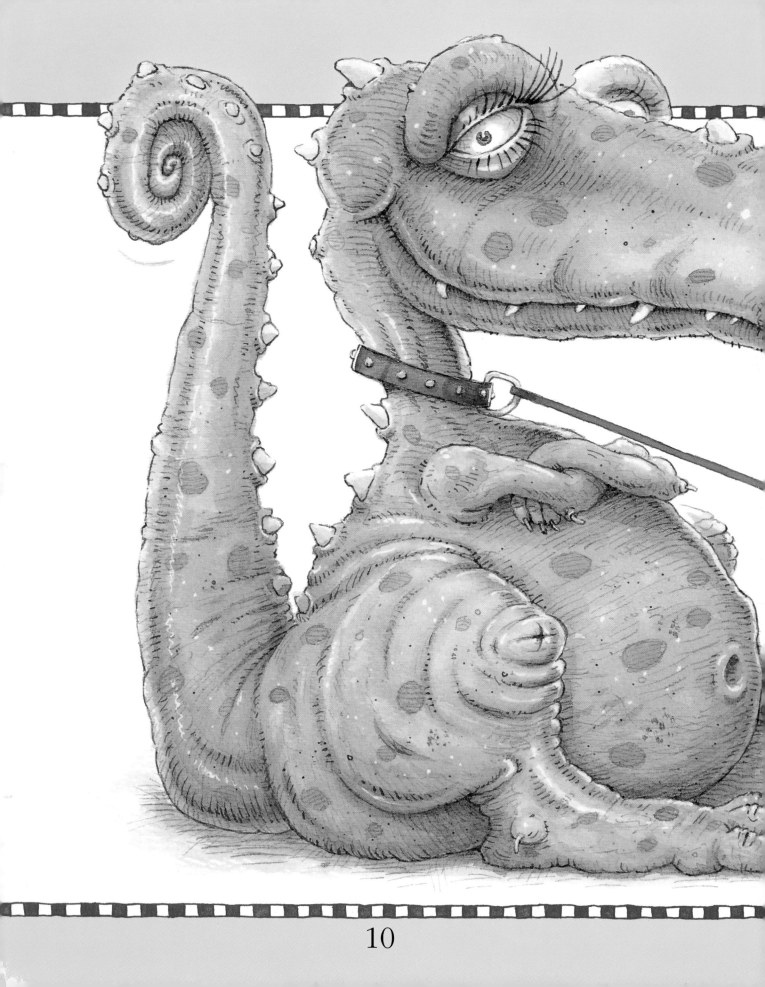

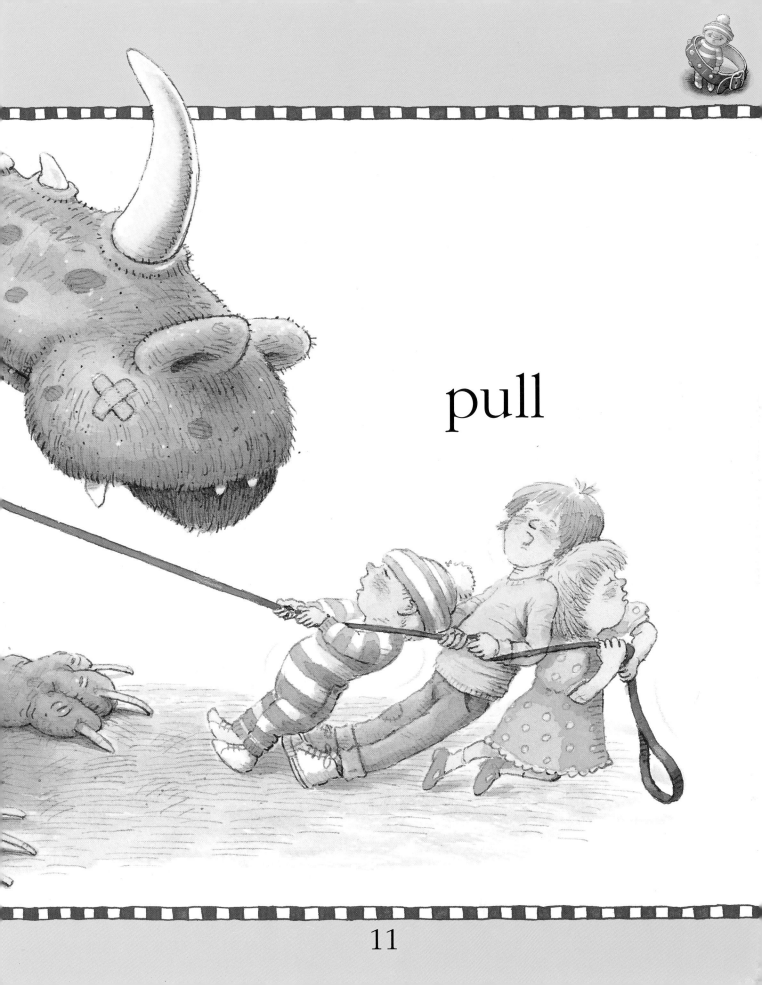

pull

and
push

CAR + CAR

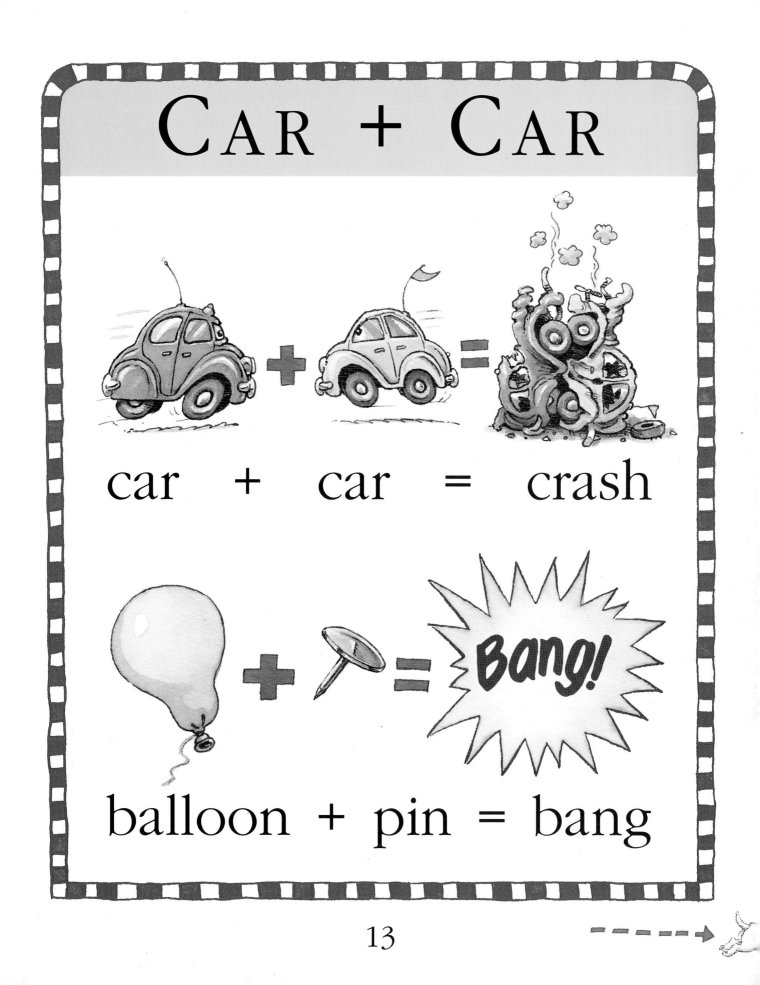

car + car = crash

balloon + pin = bang

elephant + water = squirt

I can brush my teeth.

So can I!

I can write my name.

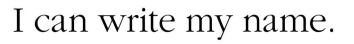

So can I!

I can read a book.

I can carry the shopping.

So can I!

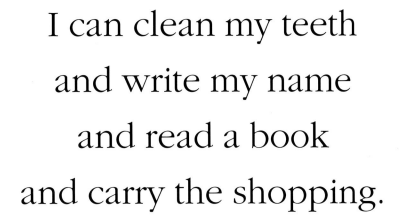

I can clean my teeth
and write my name
and read a book
and carry the shopping.

BIG HEAD

big head   little head

big ear   little ear

big eye   little eye

big nose   little nose

big mouth   little mouth

little hat…

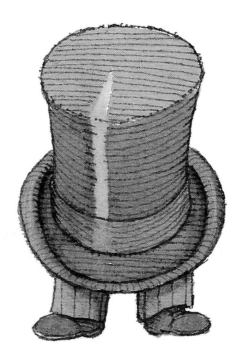

big hat

In Shirley's sweet shop

there are:

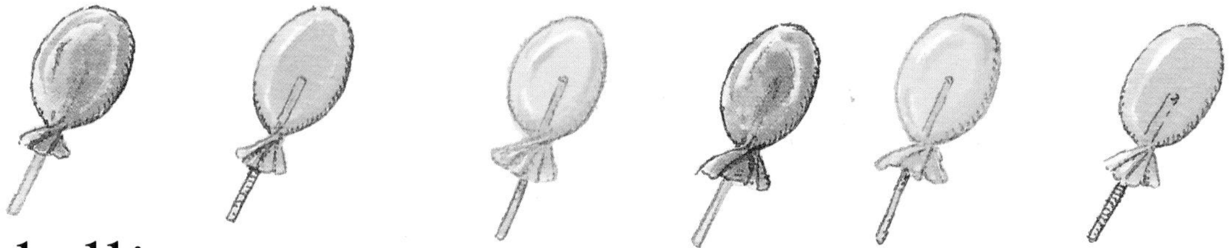

6 lollipops

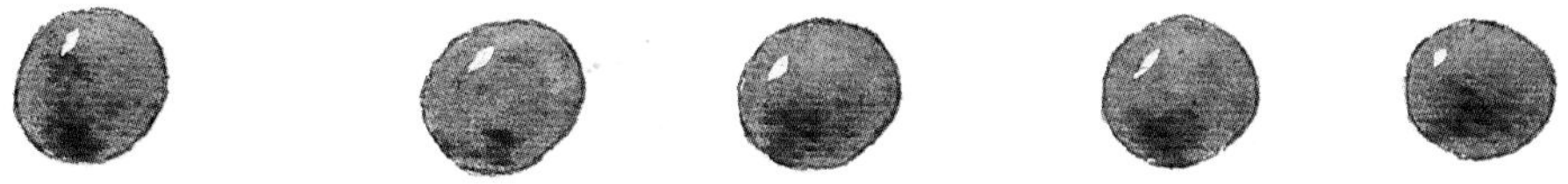

5 chocolate buttons

4 toffees

3 jelly babies

2 Smarties

1 bubble-gum

… and no customers!

Yum yum!

In Shirley's dog shop
there are:

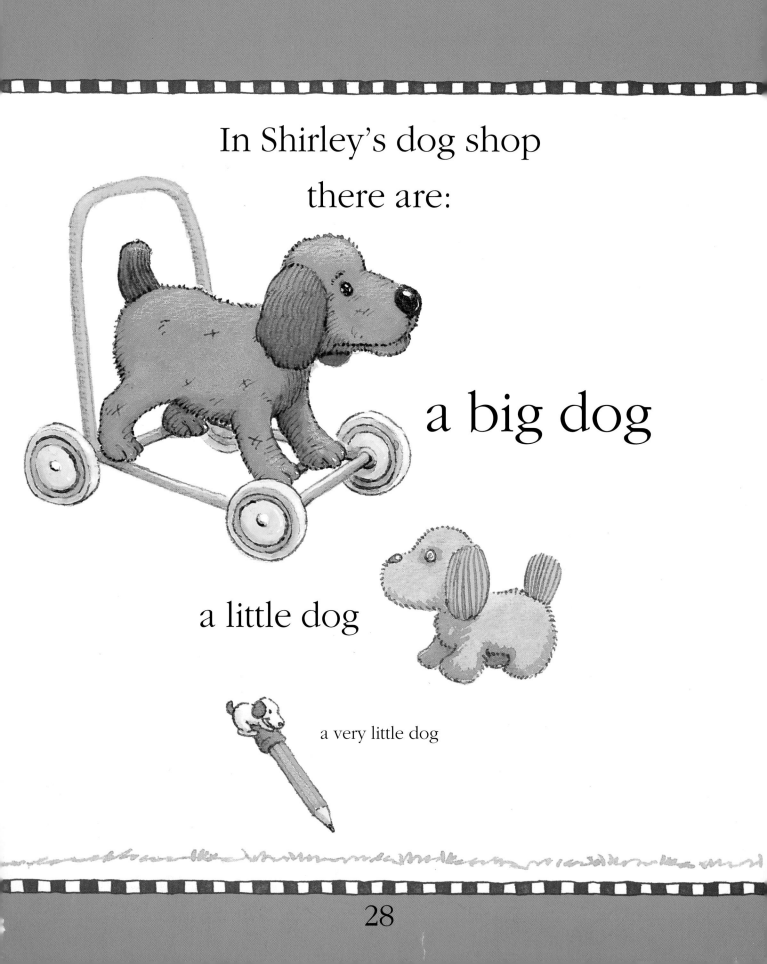

a big dog

a little dog

a very little dog

a round dog

a square dog

two spotty dogs ...

I'm off!

and a hot dog!

In Shirley's honey shop
there are pots of honey ...

In Shirley's weather shop
there are …

rain

fog

snow

wind

blue skies and sunny periods

In Shirley's tea shop

there are:

cups and plates

knives, forks and spoons

cakes and biscuits

crisps and sandwiches

fizzy drink ...

and a few friends.

BOY + BOY

boy + boy + boy + boy

+ boy + boy + boy + boy

+ boy + boy + boy + boy

+ boy + boy + boy =

a pile of boys

before the haircut

after the haircut

before the game

after the game

before the bath

after the bath

before bedtime...

...and after

the end